# ADVENT

on the lookout for hope, peace, joy, and love

written and illustrated by

Kate Ester Johnston

This book is dedicated to my best friend, Ana Lincoln,
who continually gives me the encouragement to follow my dreams
and keep growing into the person God created me to be.

ISBN 979-8-35093-012-2

# An Advent Invitation:

Waiting for Christmas can be hard especially with all of the decorations and advertisements around us. As Christians, we spend the weeks before Christmas in a season called Advent. In some churches, the colors change to purple and in some to blue, some have special wreaths pulled out, special songs that you do or don't sing, or special traditions that get added to worship. Despite some differences, it is always a time where we WAIT together so we can prepare ourselves for Christ's birth.

We practice waiting with God because there are a lot of seasons and times in our lives where we will need to know how to wait with God—where we need to be on the lookout for where God is and what God is doing while we're waiting. We'll practice that together this season as you read a page every day of the Advent season. We'll practice it as we wait to flip the page for the next day and we'll practice on each page as we look for the words HOPE, PEACE, JOY, and LOVE hidden in every picture. These are the same words that we'll focus on during the four weeks of Advent.

Because Advent can be a different amount of days every year (even though Christmas day stays the same), I've included a page for every day on the longest year of Advent. On the shorter years, you might get to catch up by reading two a day in the first or last week to stay on track.

Keep a Bible close by so you can practice finding and reading the whole scripture listed. If you don't know where the book is, find the Table of Contents in your Bible so you can get to the right book, chapter, and verses. Don't hesitate to ask for help…that's how we all get better at navigating the Bible. Some days will even have a special hymn that we'll look closely at while we wait.

Let's journey together this year, and in the years ahead, as we spend our Advent season focused on God's hope, peace, joy, and love--
waiting together for the birth of Christ.

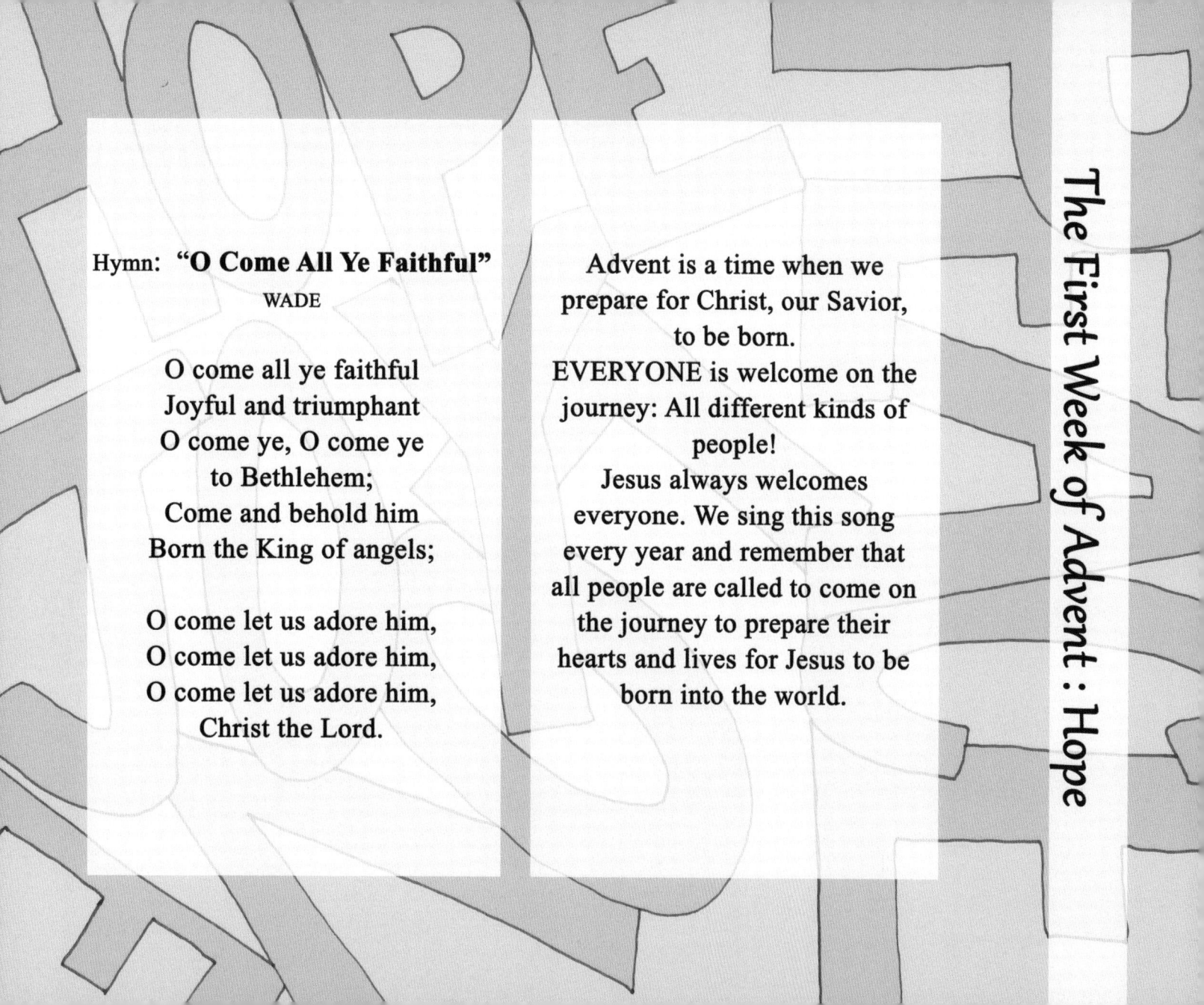

Hymn: **"O Come All Ye Faithful"**

WADE

O come all ye faithful
Joyful and triumphant
O come ye, O come ye
to Bethlehem;
Come and behold him
Born the King of angels;

O come let us adore him,
O come let us adore him,
O come let us adore him,
Christ the Lord.

Advent is a time when we
prepare for Christ, our Savior,
to be born.
EVERYONE is welcome on the
journey: All different kinds of
people!
Jesus always welcomes
everyone. We sing this song
every year and remember that
all people are called to come on
the journey to prepare their
hearts and lives for Jesus to be
born into the world.

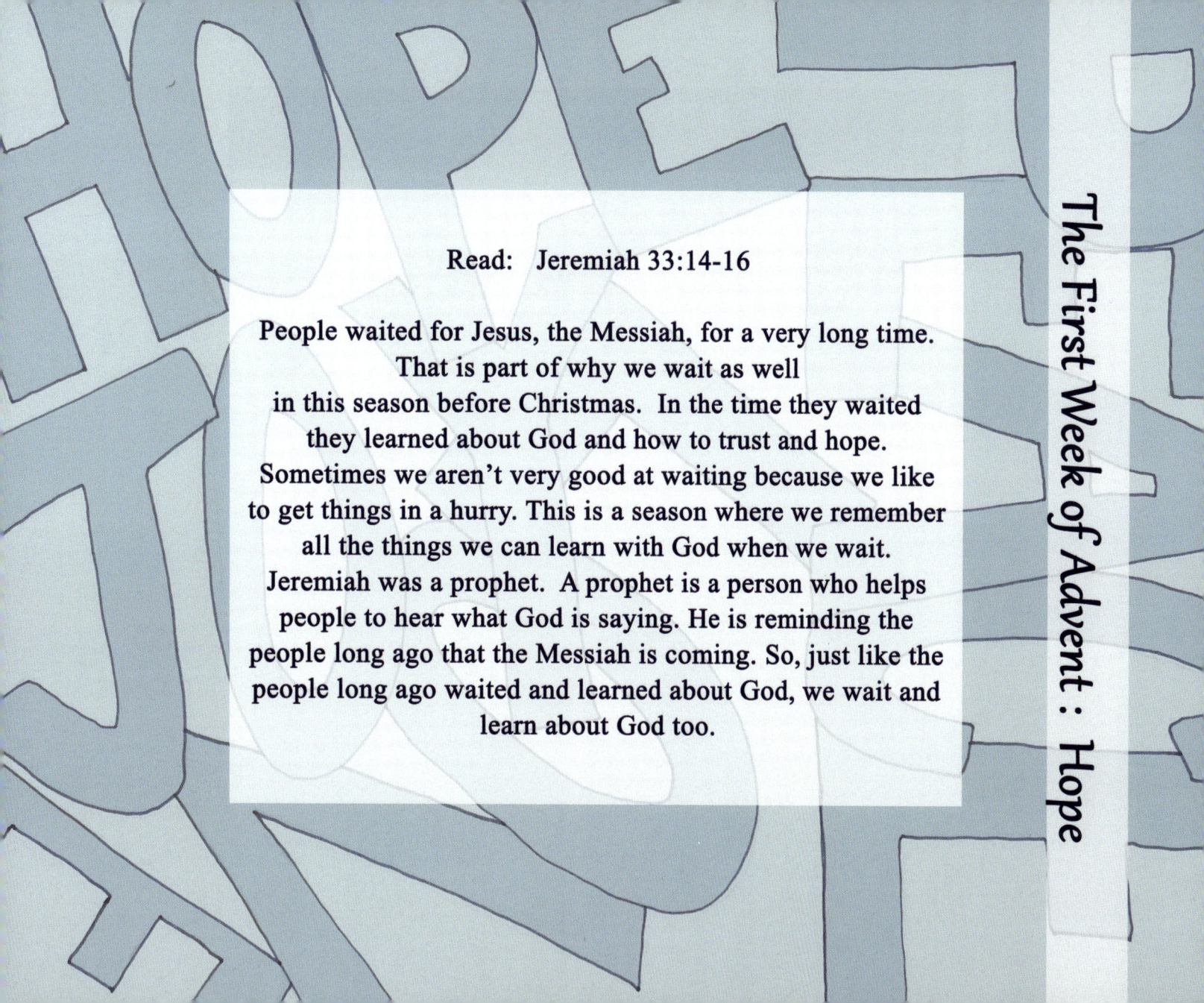

Read:    Jeremiah 33:14-16

People waited for Jesus, the Messiah, for a very long time.
That is part of why we wait as well
in this season before Christmas.  In the time they waited
they learned about God and how to trust and hope.
Sometimes we aren't very good at waiting because we like
to get things in a hurry. This is a season where we remember
all the things we can learn with God when we wait.
Jeremiah was a prophet.  A prophet is a person who helps
people to hear what God is saying. He is reminding the
people long ago that the Messiah is coming. So, just like the
people long ago waited and learned about God, we wait and
learn about God too.

The First Week of Advent : Hope

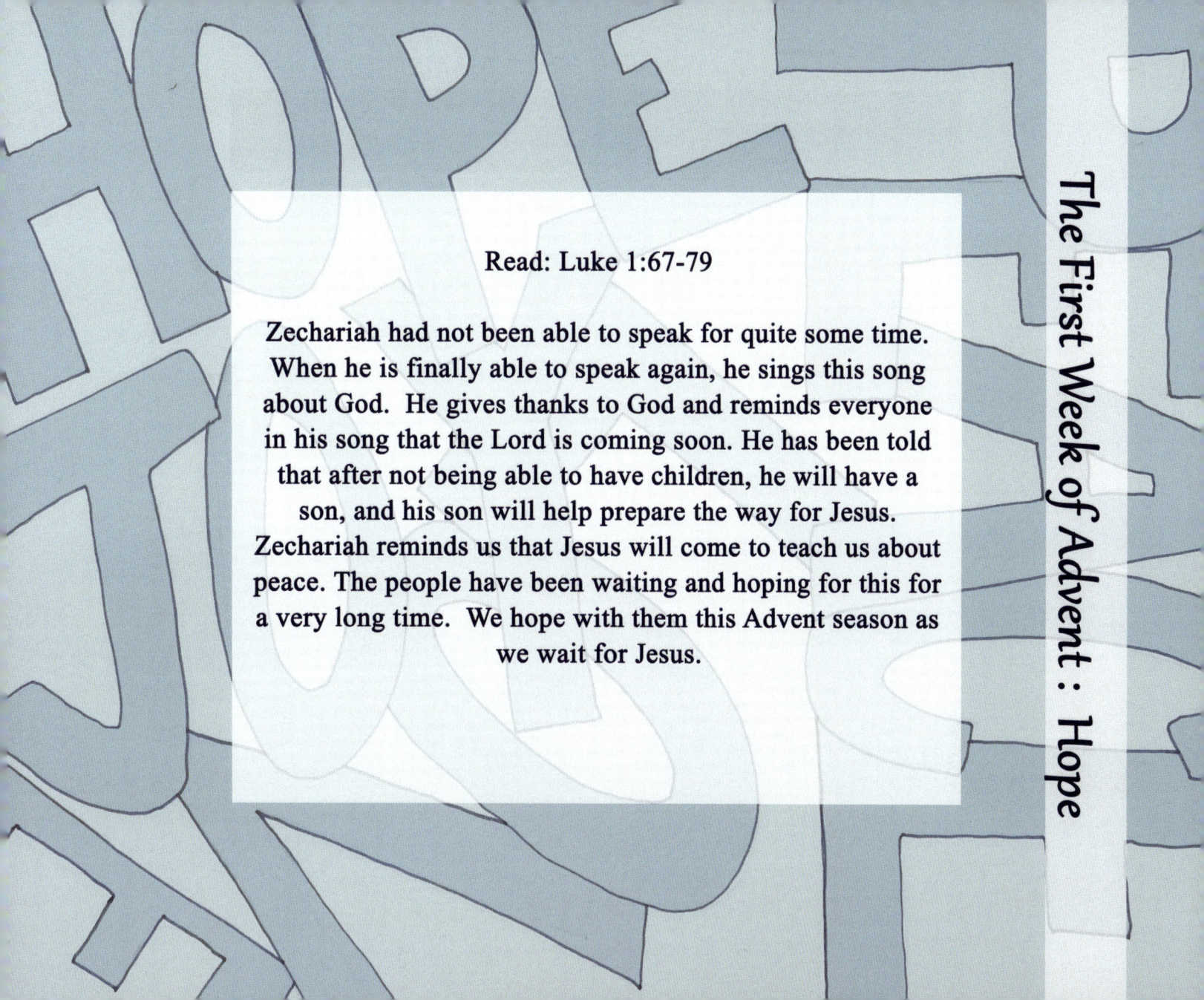

Read: Luke 1:67-79

Zechariah had not been able to speak for quite some time. When he is finally able to speak again, he sings this song about God. He gives thanks to God and reminds everyone in his song that the Lord is coming soon. He has been told that after not being able to have children, he will have a son, and his son will help prepare the way for Jesus. Zechariah reminds us that Jesus will come to teach us about peace. The people have been waiting and hoping for this for a very long time. We hope with them this Advent season as we wait for Jesus.

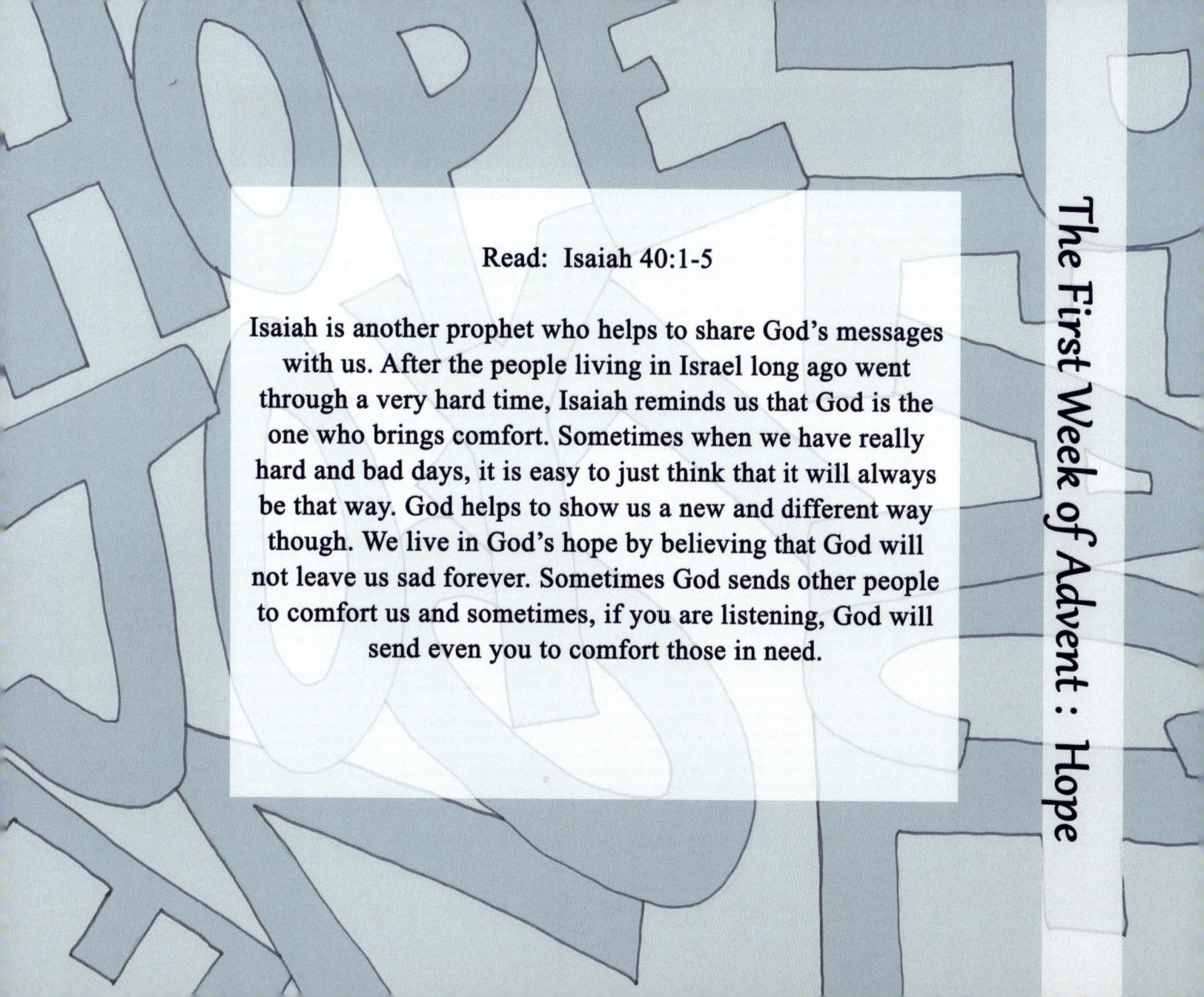

Read: Isaiah 40:1-5

Isaiah is another prophet who helps to share God's messages with us. After the people living in Israel long ago went through a very hard time, Isaiah reminds us that God is the one who brings comfort. Sometimes when we have really hard and bad days, it is easy to just think that it will always be that way. God helps to show us a new and different way though. We live in God's hope by believing that God will not leave us sad forever. Sometimes God sends other people to comfort us and sometimes, if you are listening, God will send even you to comfort those in need.

The First Week of Advent : Hope

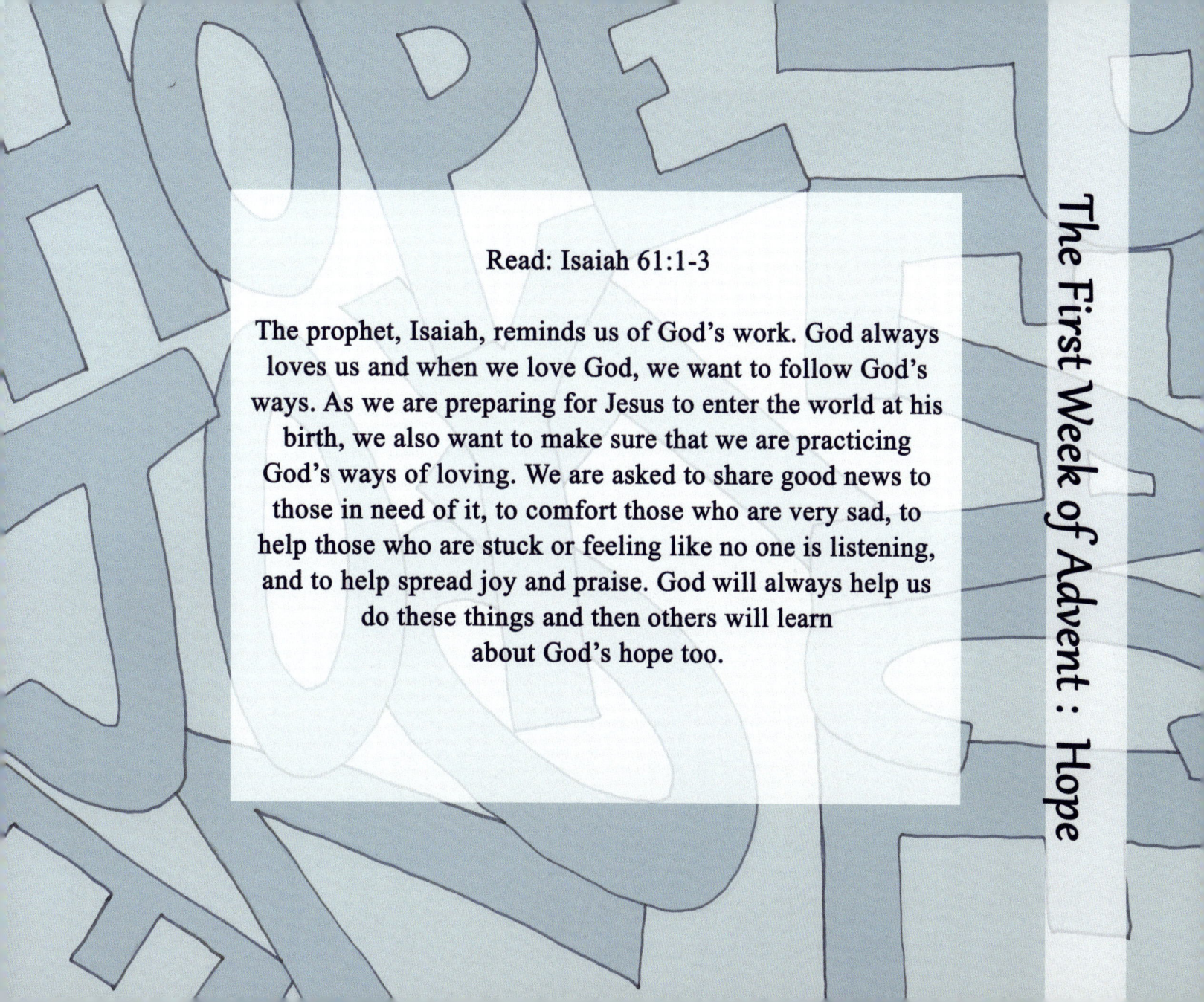

Read: Isaiah 61:1-3

The prophet, Isaiah, reminds us of God's work. God always loves us and when we love God, we want to follow God's ways. As we are preparing for Jesus to enter the world at his birth, we also want to make sure that we are practicing God's ways of loving. We are asked to share good news to those in need of it, to comfort those who are very sad, to help those who are stuck or feeling like no one is listening, and to help spread joy and praise. God will always help us do these things and then others will learn about God's hope too.

The First Week of Advent : Hope

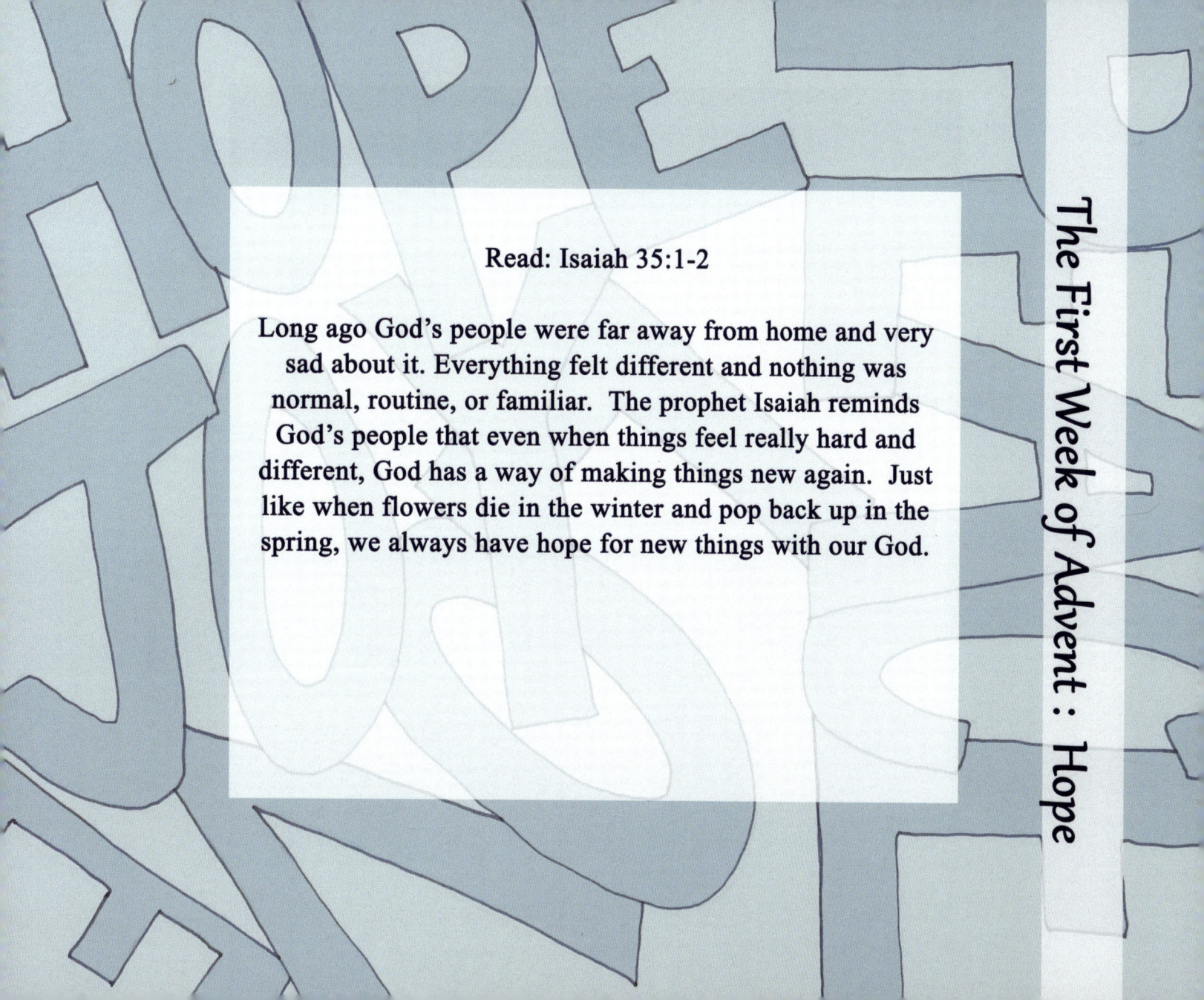

Read: Isaiah 35:1-2

Long ago God's people were far away from home and very sad about it. Everything felt different and nothing was normal, routine, or familiar.  The prophet Isaiah reminds God's people that even when things feel really hard and different, God has a way of making things new again.  Just like when flowers die in the winter and pop back up in the spring, we always have hope for new things with our God.

The First Week of Advent : Hope

## Hymn: "Come Thou Long Expected Jesus"

WESLEY

Come, Thou long expected Jesus.
Born to set Thy people free; From
our fears and sins release us,
Let us find our rest in Thee.
Israel's strength and consolation,
Hope of all the earth Thou art;
Dear desire of every nation, Joy
of every longing heart.
Born Thy people to deliver,
Born a child and yet a King,
Born to reign in us forever,
Now Thy gracious
kingdom bring.
By Thine own eternal Spirit
Rule in all our hearts alone;
By Thine all sufficient merit,
Raise us to Thy glorious throne.

This is a song we sing in
church every Advent to remind
us that we are waiting for Jesus.
It can be easy to get caught up
in presents and everything else
going on at Christmas time.
However, this song reminds us
that we are waiting for our true
hope and joy. Jesus came to
deliver every one of us which
means he came to forgive every
one of us. That is why we give
so much thanks and have so
much celebrating to do.

The First Week of Advent : Hope

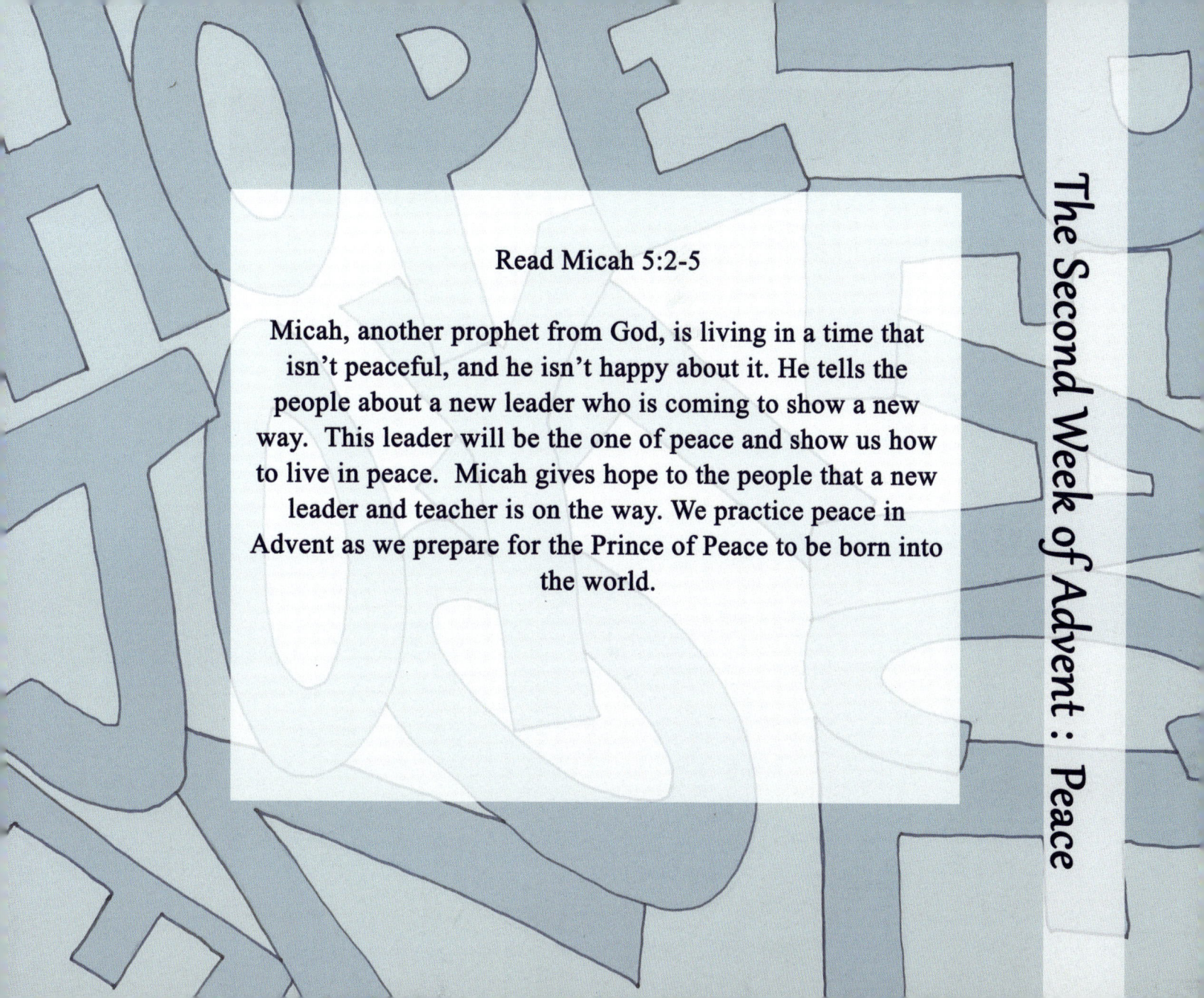

**Read Micah 5:2-5**

Micah, another prophet from God, is living in a time that isn't peaceful, and he isn't happy about it. He tells the people about a new leader who is coming to show a new way. This leader will be the one of peace and show us how to live in peace. Micah gives hope to the people that a new leader and teacher is on the way. We practice peace in Advent as we prepare for the Prince of Peace to be born into the world.

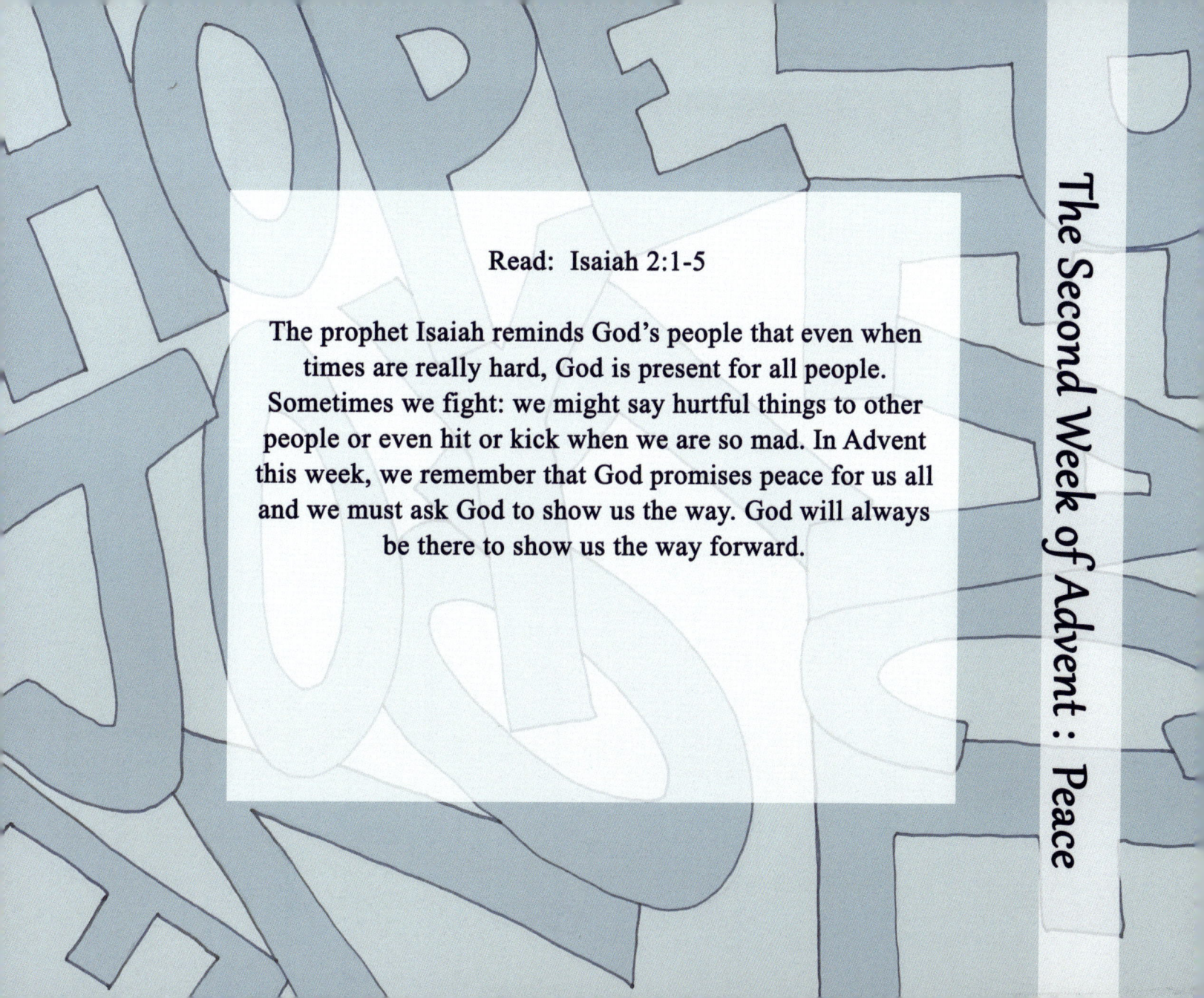

Read:  Isaiah 2:1-5

The prophet Isaiah reminds God's people that even when times are really hard, God is present for all people. Sometimes we fight: we might say hurtful things to other people or even hit or kick when we are so mad. In Advent this week, we remember that God promises peace for us all and we must ask God to show us the way. God will always be there to show us the way forward.

The Second Week of Advent : Peace

## Hymn: **"Comfort, Comfort You My People"**

OLEARIUS

Comfort, comfort you my people, speak of peace, thus says our God; comfort those who sit in darkness bowed beneath oppression's load. Speak you to Jerusalem of the peace that waits for them; tell them that their sins I cover, and their warfare now is over.

Make you straight what long was crooked, make the rougher places plain; let your hearts be true and humble, as befits God's holy reign, for the glory of the Lord Now o'er earth is shed abroad, and all flesh shall see the token that God's word is never broken.

This is another song that we sing every Advent in church because it reminds us that God is able to make things new. When we have messed up or are afraid, God is able to keep loving us and helping us live in love with others. God promises to always love us and God's word is never broken.

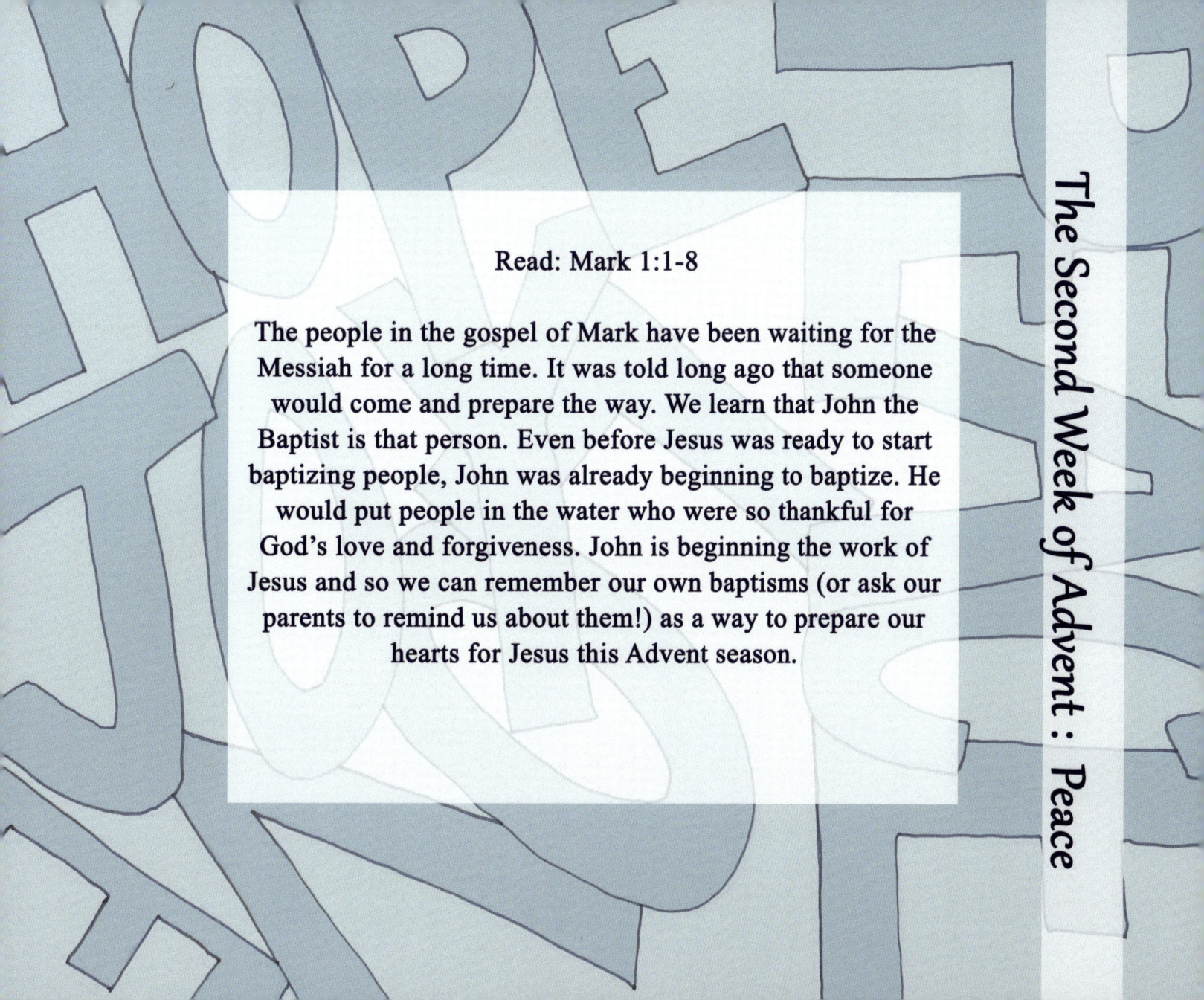

**Read: Mark 1:1-8**

The people in the gospel of Mark have been waiting for the Messiah for a long time. It was told long ago that someone would come and prepare the way. We learn that John the Baptist is that person. Even before Jesus was ready to start baptizing people, John was already beginning to baptize. He would put people in the water who were so thankful for God's love and forgiveness. John is beginning the work of Jesus and so we can remember our own baptisms (or ask our parents to remind us about them!) as a way to prepare our hearts for Jesus this Advent season.

The Second Week of Advent : Peace

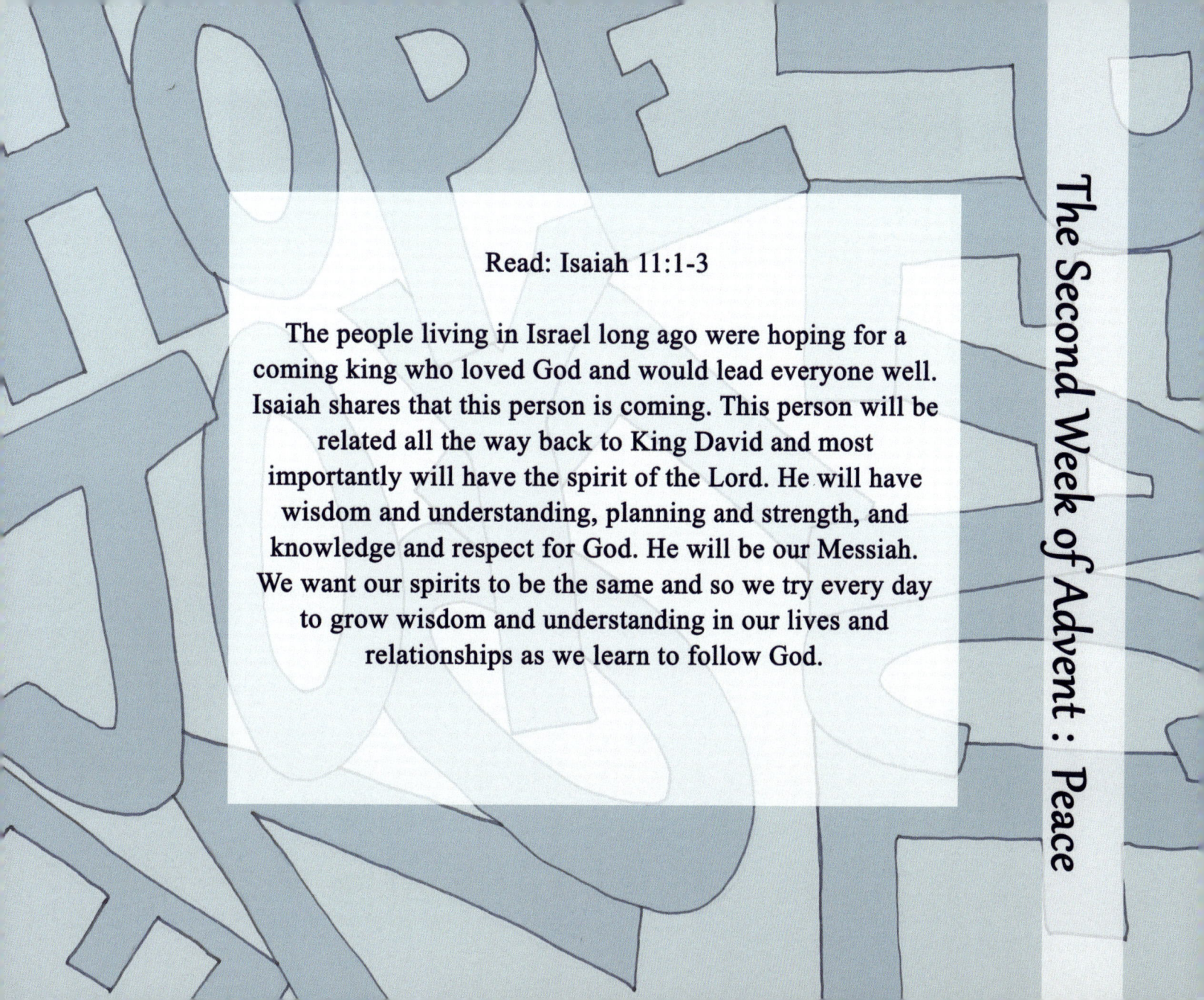

Read: Isaiah 11:1-3

The people living in Israel long ago were hoping for a coming king who loved God and would lead everyone well. Isaiah shares that this person is coming. This person will be related all the way back to King David and most importantly will have the spirit of the Lord. He will have wisdom and understanding, planning and strength, and knowledge and respect for God. He will be our Messiah. We want our spirits to be the same and so we try every day to grow wisdom and understanding in our lives and relationships as we learn to follow God.

The Second Week of Advent : Peace

Read: Isaiah 11:6-10

We know that the Messiah who is coming is going to have the spirit of the Lord. Because of this spirit and who this person is, we know that a whole new way of living is about to happen. This Messiah is going to be able to bring peace to the world in a way that we have never known. Can you imagine a leopard and goat living happily together? Sometimes it is hard for us to just imagine living peaceably with our sibling and friends. This new King will show us how to live in the way of peace with everyone if we keep choosing to listen to our God.

## Hymn: "It Came Upon the Midnight Clear"

SEARS

It came upon the midnight clear
That glorious song of old
From angels bending near the earth
To touch their harps of gold
Peace on the earth, good will to all
From heaven's all-gracious King
The world in solemn stillness lay
To hear the angels sing
For lo, the days are hastening on
By prophets seen of old
When with the ever-circling years
Shall come the time foretold
When peace shall over all the earth
It's ancient splendors fling
And the whole world give back the song
Which now the angels sing

This is a song that we sing in church at Christmas time: for some churches during Advent and for some churches after Advent. It helps us to remember that Jesus has loved people long before us. That means that Jesus has loved more people than we can even imagine, and Jesus will love all the people after us too. That is a lot of people! The prophets long ago told of a Messiah who would come to bring peace and teach us forgiveness. Even the angels sing and remind us of that. We can all sing too because God is teaching us about peace and has love for everyone that never ends.

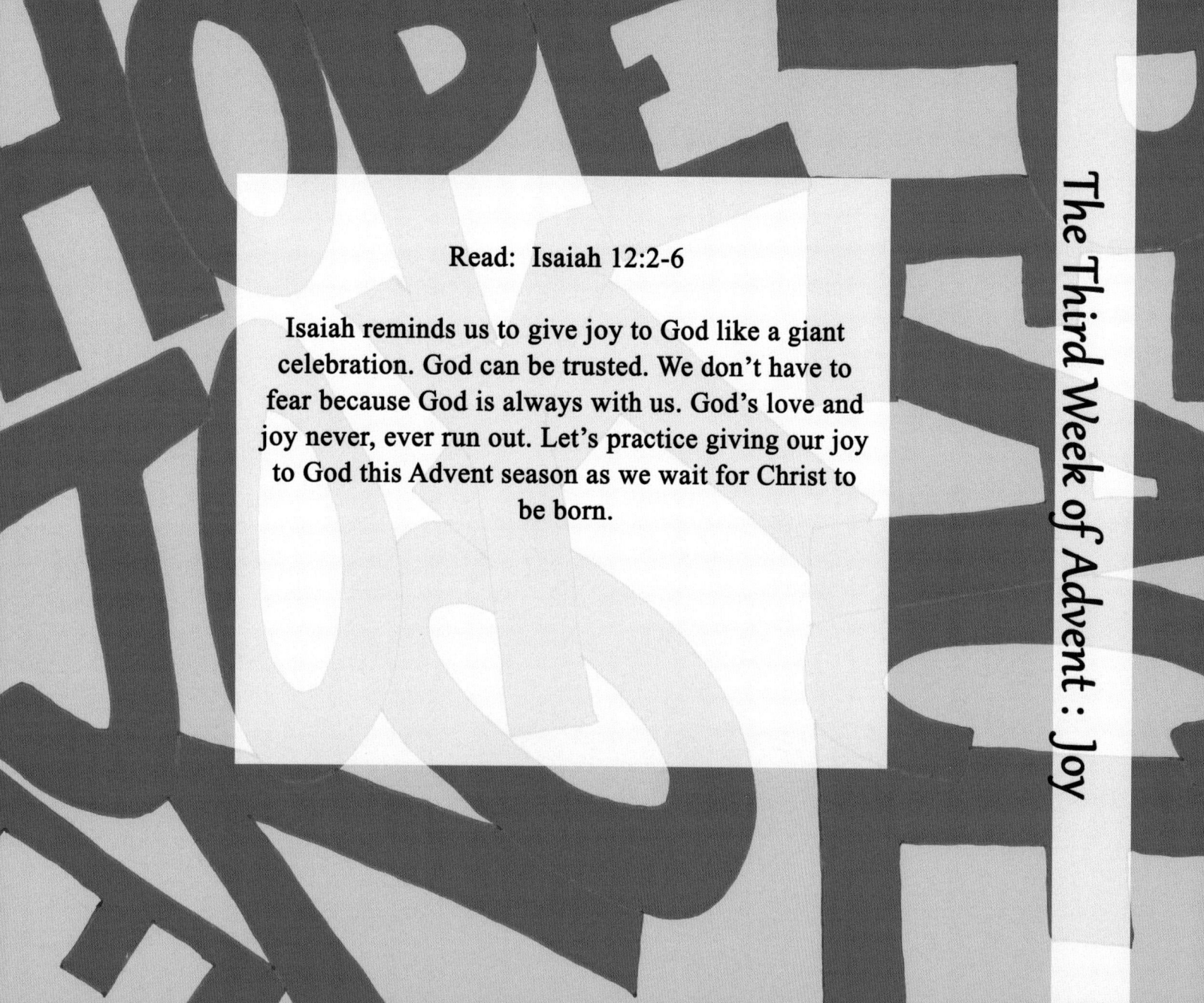

Read: Isaiah 12:2-6

Isaiah reminds us to give joy to God like a giant celebration. God can be trusted. We don't have to fear because God is always with us. God's love and joy never, ever run out. Let's practice giving our joy to God this Advent season as we wait for Christ to be born.

## Hymn: "O Come, O Come Emmanuel"

### NEALE

O come, O come, Emmanuel,
And ransom captive Israel,
That mourns in lonely
exile here
Until the Son of God appear,
Rejoice! Rejoice! Emmanuel
Shall come to thee, O Israel.
O come, thou Dayspring,
Come and cheer
Our spirits by thine
advent here;
Disperse the gloomy
clouds of night,
And death's dark shadows
put to flight
Rejoice! Rejoice!
Emmanuel shall come
to thee, O Israel.

This is a song we sing in church every Advent that reminds us that even when things are really hard, we can still rejoice because God is with us. Some days that is really difficult to remember. It is okay to cry, be angry, or frustrated. We prepare our hearts for Jesus coming by letting God in when we are feeling those emotions and trusting that God will help to heal our feelings so we can feel joy again.

The Third Week of Advent : Joy

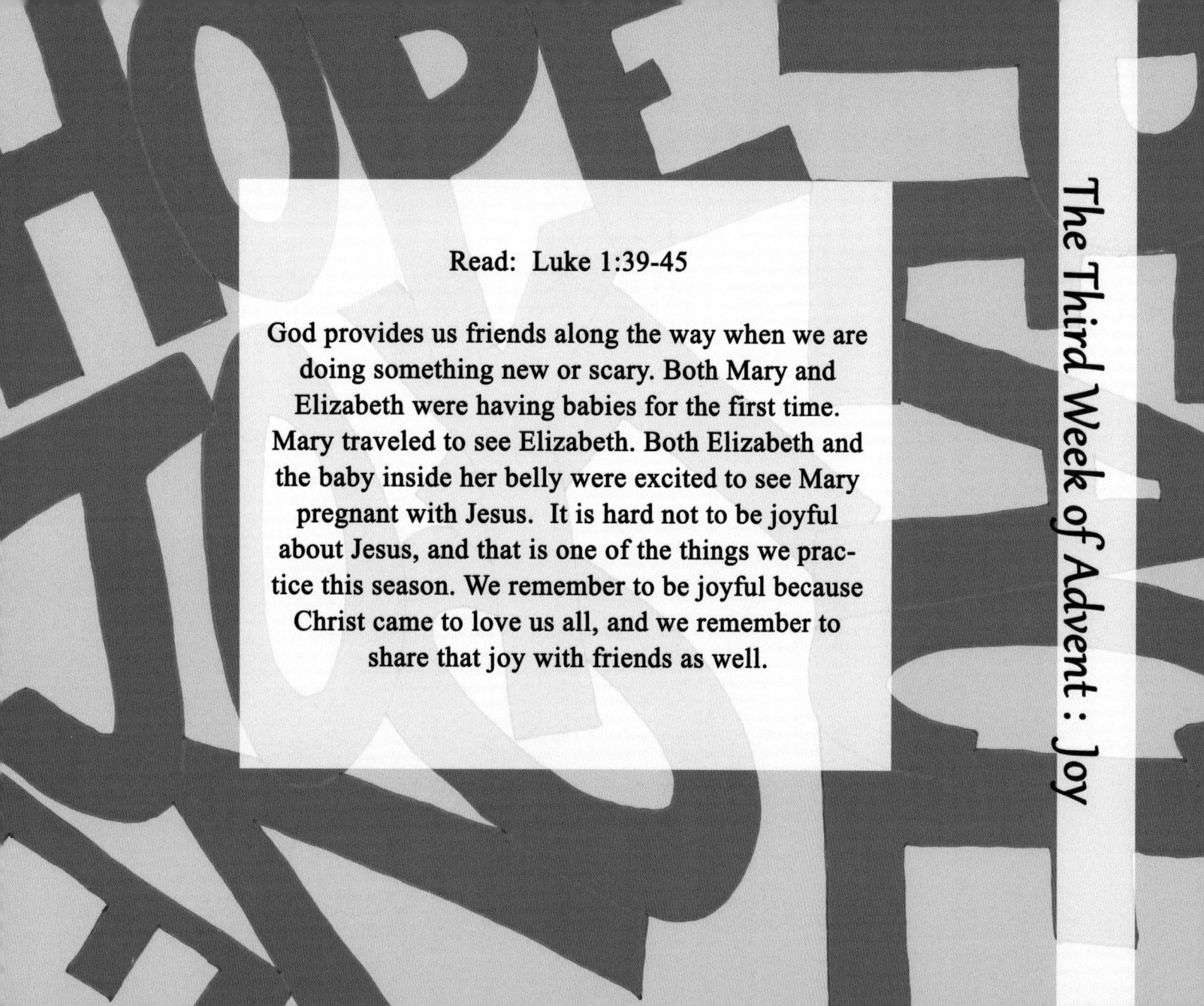

Read: Luke 1:39-45

God provides us friends along the way when we are doing something new or scary. Both Mary and Elizabeth were having babies for the first time. Mary traveled to see Elizabeth. Both Elizabeth and the baby inside her belly were excited to see Mary pregnant with Jesus. It is hard not to be joyful about Jesus, and that is one of the things we practice this season. We remember to be joyful because Christ came to love us all, and we remember to share that joy with friends as well.

## Hymn: "What Child Is This?"

DIX

What child is this, who, laid to rest,
On Mary's lap is sleeping?
Whom angels greet with anthems
sweet, while shepherds watch
are keeping?
This, this is Christ the King,
Whom shepherds guard and angels
sing: Haste, haste to bring Him
laud, the babe, the son of Mary.
So bring him incense, gold, and
myrrh. Come, peasant, king, to own
him. The King of Kings salvation
brings, let loving hearts enthrone
him.
This, this is Christ the King,
Whom shepherds guard and angels
sing: Haste, haste to bring Him
laud, the babe, the son of Mary.

We sing this song in church
every year to remind us that
we are giving thanks for the
birth of Jesus. While Jesus
was born human, like you
and me, he was also born
God. Shepherds and Magi
went to give thanks for his
life and birth. The rich and
poor, people near and far,
every kind of person was
welcome to celebrate his
birth. As we prepare for
Christ, we are joyful that
everyone is loved by Jesus!

The Third Week of Advent : Joy

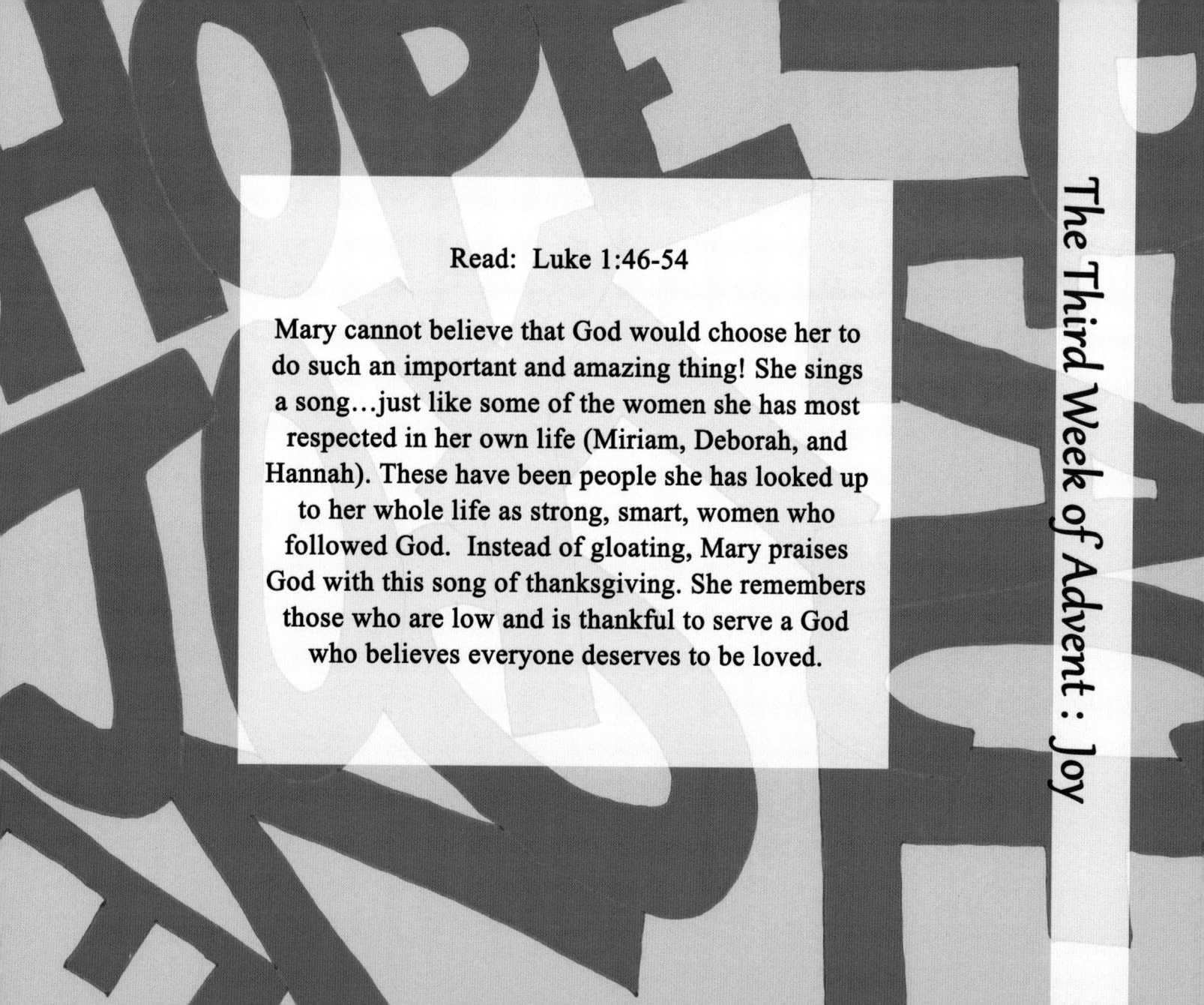

Read: Luke 1:46-54

Mary cannot believe that God would choose her to do such an important and amazing thing! She sings a song…just like some of the women she has most respected in her own life (Miriam, Deborah, and Hannah). These have been people she has looked up to her whole life as strong, smart, women who followed God.  Instead of gloating, Mary praises God with this song of thanksgiving. She remembers those who are low and is thankful to serve a God who believes everyone deserves to be loved.

## Hymn: "Let All Mortal Flesh Keep Silence"

MOULTRIE

Let all mortal flesh keep silence,
And with fear and trembling
stand;
Ponder nothing earthly-minded,
for with blessing in his hand,
Christ our God to earth
descendeth,
our full homage to demand.
At his feet the six-winged seraph,
Cherubim, with sleepless eye,
Veil their faces to the presence,
As with ceaseless voice they cry;
Alleluia, Alleluia, Alleluia,
Lord Most High!

We sing this song in church every year at Advent to remember that God chose to come from heaven to earth to be with us. God chose to be born a human in order to help us learn to love better. That is why we praise God so much. Even the angels can't help singing 'Alleluia' around Jesus.

Read: Isaiah 9:2, 6

Sometimes the dark scares us because we fear what we do not know...and it can be hard to know what is around you without any light. The prophet, Isaiah, is reminding us that the Messiah's birth will be like shining a light in the darkness. It will help us understand the darkness better so that we can see the good in both the light and dark spaces. God grows us in all seasons.

We can celebrate and be joyful because Christ is coming as a light into our world...this light will better help us learn, grow, and see God in all of the unknown.

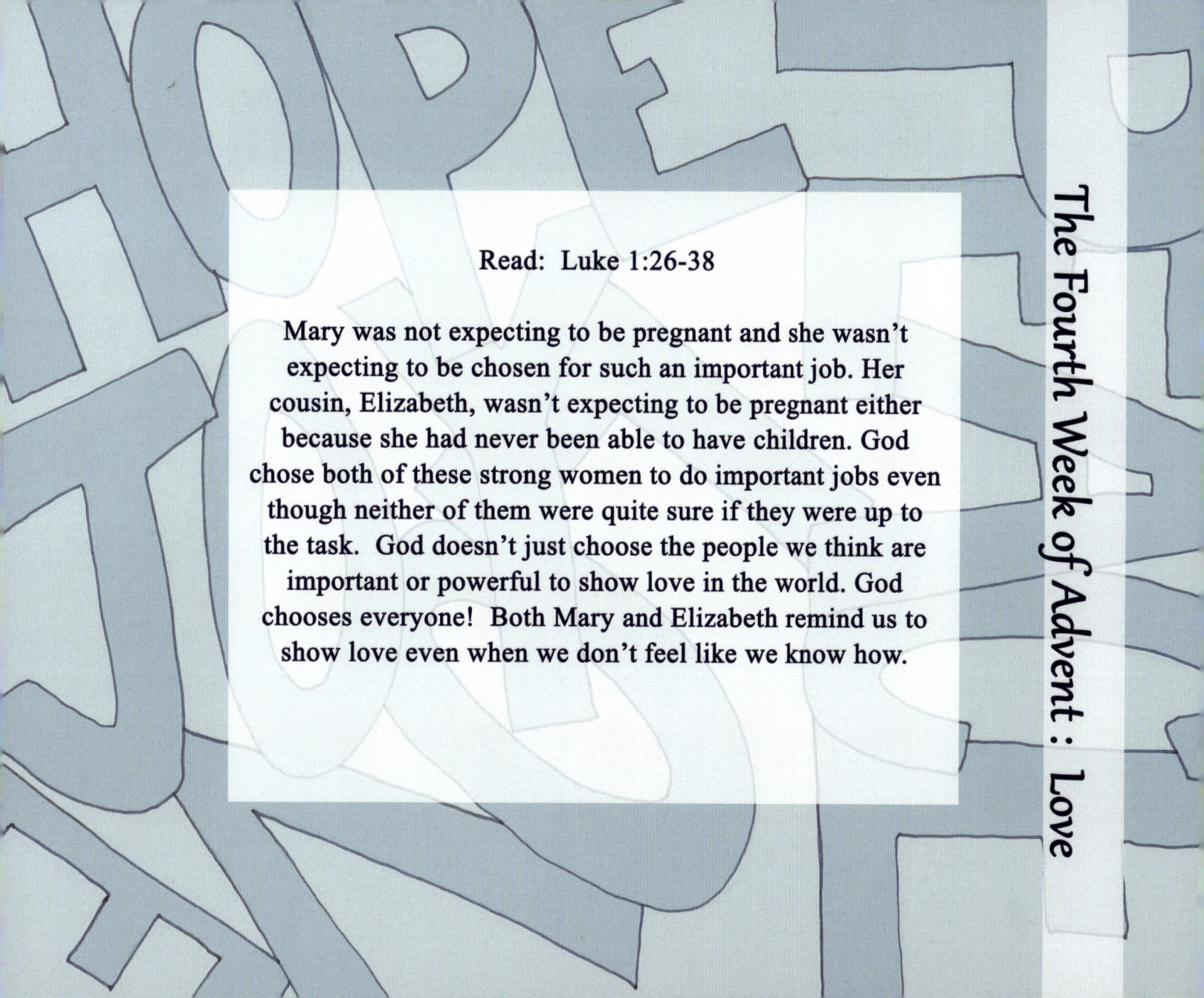

Read: Luke 1:26-38

Mary was not expecting to be pregnant and she wasn't expecting to be chosen for such an important job. Her cousin, Elizabeth, wasn't expecting to be pregnant either because she had never been able to have children. God chose both of these strong women to do important jobs even though neither of them were quite sure if they were up to the task. God doesn't just choose the people we think are important or powerful to show love in the world. God chooses everyone! Both Mary and Elizabeth remind us to show love even when we don't feel like we know how.

The Fourth Week of Advent : Love

Read: Matthew 1:18-25

An Angel came to tell Joseph to be loving and kind to Mary when he was really confused. The messenger told Joseph that Mary would have a son and the baby being born would mean that God was with us forever and ever. Joseph chose to listen to God and trust God. This is something all of us can work on during Advent while we prepare our hearts for the birth of Jesus.

The Fourth Week of Advent : Love

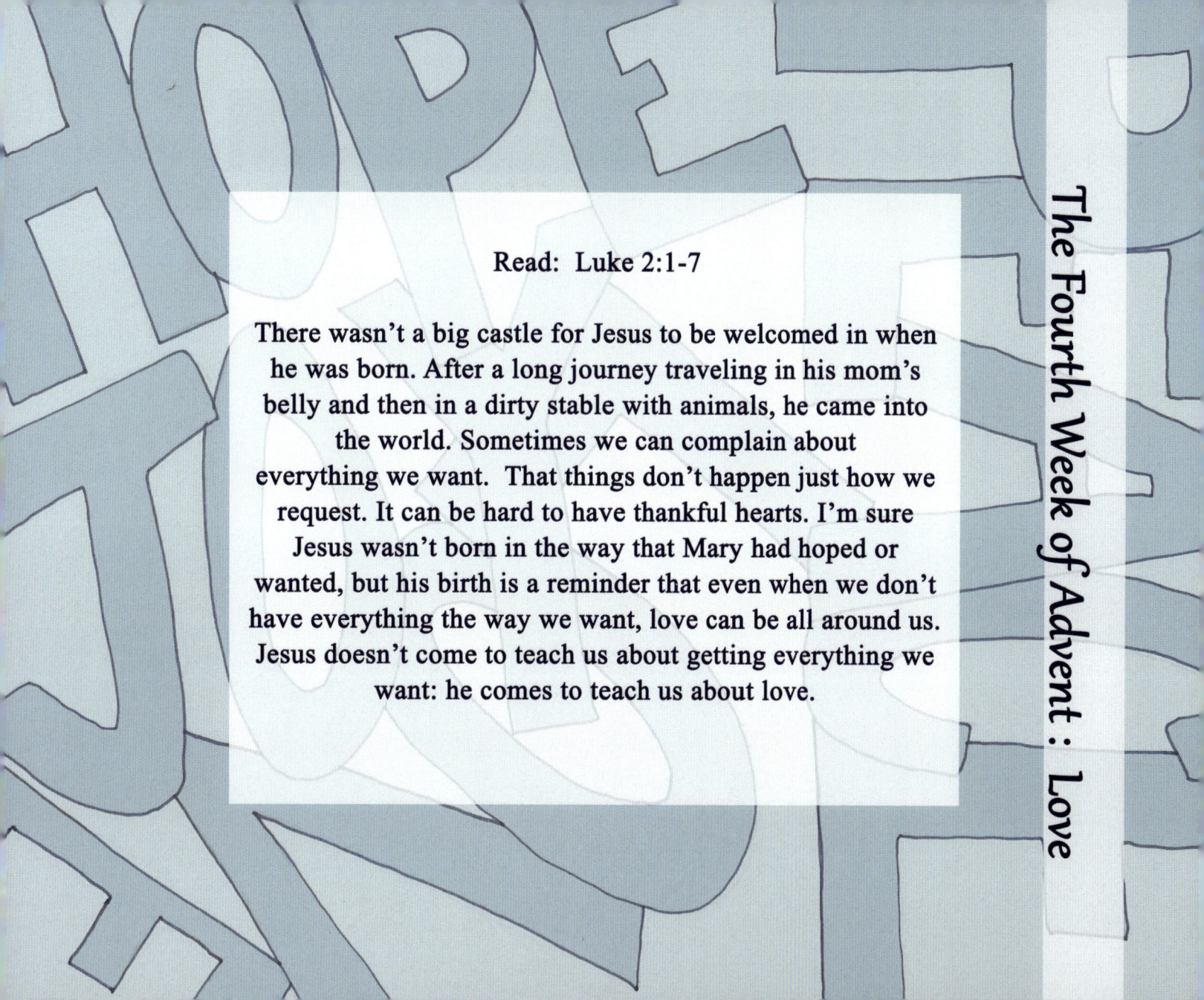

Read:  Luke 2:1-7

There wasn't a big castle for Jesus to be welcomed in when he was born. After a long journey traveling in his mom's belly and then in a dirty stable with animals, he came into the world. Sometimes we can complain about everything we want.  That things don't happen just how we request. It can be hard to have thankful hearts. I'm sure Jesus wasn't born in the way that Mary had hoped or wanted, but his birth is a reminder that even when we don't have everything the way we want, love can be all around us. Jesus doesn't come to teach us about getting everything we want: he comes to teach us about love.

Read:  Luke 2:8-14

The news began to spread that Jesus had been born into the world. The angels shared the news first.  They didn't share the news as you might expect with all of the Kings and rulers and wealthy people first. The Angels shared the news with shepherds.  Anyone can hear God's good news.
It is the gift of love for everyone.

The Fourth Week of Advent : Love

### Hymn: "Angels We Have Heard on High"

TRADITIONAL FRENCH CAROL

Angels we have heard on high
Sweetly singing o'er the plains
And the mountains in reply
Echoing their joyous strains.
Gloria in Excelsis Deo
Gloria in Excelsis Deo
Shepherds why this jubilee?
Why your joyous
strains prolong?
What the gladsome tidings be
Which inspire your heavenly
song?
Gloria in Excelsis Deo
Gloria in Excelsis Deo

All of creation is thankful
when Christ is born. Even the
mountains sing about their joy!
Everyone is so happy that Jesus
is here and is full of love.
The angels begin to spread the
good news to all who will hear
and then we get to help to keep
spreading the good news even
today.

Read: Luke 2:15-17

The shepherds chose to believe the angels. They went and greeted this newborn King. They were so excited to meet Jesus. This is why we've waited all Advent too. We get to be excited to meet our newborn King!

The Fourth Week of Advent : Love

## Hymn: "O Holy Night"

CAPPEAU

O Holy Night
The stars are brightly shining
It is the night
of our dear Savior's birth
Long lay the world
In sin and error pining
Til he appeared
And the soul felt its worth
A thrill of hope
The weary world rejoices
For yonder breaks
a new and glorious morn
Fall on your knees
O hear the angel voices
O night divine
O night when Christ was born
O night divine
O night, O night divine

After lots of waiting, Jesus is born tonight! We feel so much hope on this night because we remember that Jesus is with every one of us. The whole world can rejoice because our Savior has been born! Give thanks for God's love tonight. You're loved more than you know by your Savior.

Christmas Eve

Read: John 1:1-14

Today Jesus is born. Joy to the whole world!
We remember today that Jesus was around long before he
was born in the world. He was in the very beginning of time
and chose to come to earth to teach us, so we could live in
his hope, peace, joy and love.  That is a really big gift!
We get to celebrate Jesus all year by following him,
showing his love to others, and learning to live in peace
with all the different people we meet.

Christmas Day